This book is dedicated to all of my friends who believed in me and never gave up. It's friends like mine that give the true meaning to this book.

THANKS DAD, TAMMY, GRANDMA, BILL, JERRY, CANDY, LIZ AND GERRY, MARK, GRANT, MICHAEL, DAWN, SANDY, SARA, ISABEL AND BENNY, MEGAN, CINDY, SUE, LINDA, KERRI AND EVERYONE AT LITTLE, BROWN AND COMPANY

Love,
Todd

First Edition

Library of Congress Cataloging-in-Publication Data

Parr, Todd.
    The best friends book / Todd Parr. — 1st ed.
        p.   cm.
    Summary: Illustrations and brief text describe how best friends treat each other.
    ISBN 0-316-69201-8
    [1. Best friends — Fiction. 2. Friendship — Fiction.] I. Title.
PZ7.P2447Be   2000
[E] — dc21   98-46961

10 9 8 7 6 5 4 3 2 1

TW

Printed in Singapore

The Best Friends Book

TODD PARR

Little, Brown and Company
Boston New York London

Best Friends
will let you jump on
their bed no matter
how big you are

Best Friends
will let you make
dinner for them even
if you serve spaghetti
and worms

Best Friends
will forgive you
even if you step
on their paw

Best Friends
will share their pizza
with you even if you
want to wear the
pepperoni

Best Friends
will visit you when
you're sick even if
you give them
BIG green spots

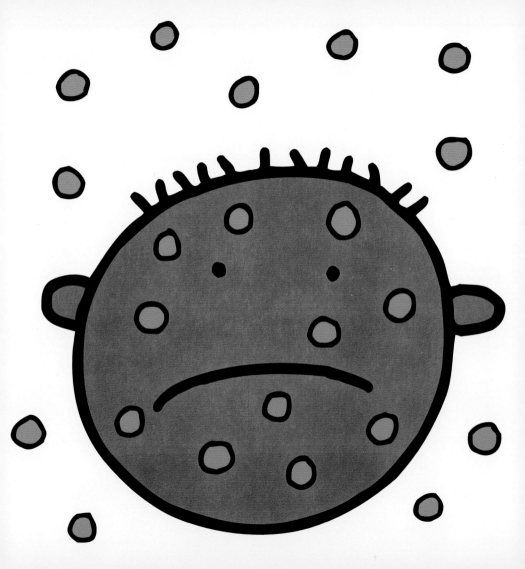

Best Friends
won't share your
secret notes even if
the teacher
catches them

Best Friends
will find you even
if you get lost

Best Friends
will say you look
good even if you
have a bad haircut

Best Friends
will tell you funny
jokes even if you
blow milk out of your
nose when you laugh

Best Friends
will let you play with
their doll even if you
pull her arm off

Best Friends
will wear the
birthday present
you gave them even
if it doesn't fit

Best Friends
will keep in touch
with you even if
you move a million
miles away